Crisis Management at the Speed of the Internet

Crisis Management at the Speed of the Internet

Trend Report

Bob Hayes
Kathleen Kotwica

AMSTERDAM • BOSTON • HEIDELBERG • LONDON
NEW YORK • OXFORD • PARIS • SAN DIEGO
SAN FRANCISCO • SINGAPORE • SYDNEY • TOKYO

ELSEVIER

Security
Executive Council

Elsevier

The Boulevard, Langford Lane, Kidlington, Oxford, OX5 1GB, UK
225 Wyman Street, Waltham, MA 02451, USA

First published 2013

Notices
Knowledge and best practice in this field are constantly changing. As new research and
experience broaden our understanding, changes in research methods, professional practices,
or medical treatment may become necessary.

Practitioners and researchers must always rely on their own experience and knowledge
in evaluating and using any information, methods, compounds, or experiments described herein.
In using such information or methods they should be mindful of their own safety and the safety
of others, including parties for whom they have a professional responsibility.

To the fullest extent of the law, neither the Publisher nor the authors, contributors, or editors,
assume any liability for any injury and/or damage to persons or property as a matter of products
liability, negligence or otherwise, or from any use or operation of any methods, products,
instructions, or ideas contained in the material herein.

British Library Cataloguing in Publication Data
A catalogue record for this book is available from the British Library

Library of Congress Cataloging-in-Publication Data
A catalog record for this book is available from the Library of Congress

ISBN: 978-0-12-411587-3

For more publications in the Elsevier Risk Management and Security
Collection, visit our website at store.elsevier.com/SecurityExecutiveCouncil.

This book has been manufactured using Print On Demand technology. Each copy is produced
to order and is limited to black ink. The online version of this book will show color figures
where appropriate.

Working together
to grow libraries in
developing countries

ELSEVIER   Book Aid International

www.elsevier.com • www.bookaid.org

CONTENTS

Executive Summary

Crisis Management at the Speed of the Internet provides security executives and practitioners with an overview of the potentially harmful impact of social media communication on corporate reputation. Isolated, un-publicized embarrassments and scandals are a thing of the past: Within minutes, the online consumer community can propel a company into an image crisis and a financial disaster—even if the viral information isn't factual. Examples of companies that have experienced this kind of threat are explored, and practical, strategic methods for mitigating and resolving a crisis are described. This report is a valuable resource to any security professional who is working to create or improve an existing corporate crisis management policy.

WHAT IS A TREND REPORT?

A trend report is a document that highlights one fast-growing trend in the fields of corporate security and risk management. Based on research, these reports help industry leaders and practitioners learn the basics of a topic of emerging importance and provide guidance and resources for applying what they've learned in a real-world environment. These reports can be utilized by mid- to upper-level security managers, instructors at institutions of higher education, or by human resources professionals in training sessions.

INTRODUCTION

Communication on the Internet—from Twitter to YouTube, Facebook to MySpace, even email, blogs, and instant messaging—is making corporate crisis management more critical than ever, especially as it relates to preserving brand equity. Communication in the Internet era moves more rapidly than ever before, yet the ramifications of quickly moving and hard-to-control information are often not well understood by corporate management. The viral nature of the Internet can enable information—both positive and negative—about a company or brand to be rapidly disseminated to huge numbers of recipients within seconds.

In the new climate of viral videos and unbridled blogs, anyone anywhere can create a corporate crisis, even with no access to company resources and no inside knowledge of the company; they may be disgruntled former employees with an axe to grind, or just kids who think they're being funny. Even if their claims are untrue, negative commentary and information can be accepted as fact and can easily become part of the popular culture. It can exist for weeks, months, or years after it is posted, and often it's hard for a company to have such posts removed from a social network site. If information is not balanced or challenged, many people will be unable to determine whether it is accurate or not.

Damage to a company's reputation resulting from harmful YouTube videos, tweets, or venomous rumors spread on Facebook can impact the organization's stock price and destroy millions of dollars in brand equity. Dozens of companies have already been damaged this way, and more face a greater likelihood of harm every day. Unfortunately, corporate strategies to address crisis management have not kept up well with these newer media, and many corporations are ill-prepared to respond when a brand image crisis hits. Their communications processes may be mired in organizational bureaucracy, or tied to outdated public relations strategies. Most important, they are likely to respond too slowly to really address the problem.

This report sheds light on the rapidly changing nature of brand image threats on the Internet and how companies can respond strategically. Specifically, the report will:

- **Provide understanding of the newer Internet communication tools:** How are YouTube, Twitter, Facebook, MySpace and other communication formats different from traditional mass communication media, and what is the possible impact of those differences?
- **Provide examples of companies that have faced threats to their brands and how they have responded:** What can today's risk management practitioners learn from these experiences?
- **Describe strategies to prepare and help mitigate the effects when a crisis occurs:** Existing ways to responding to a crisis don't necessarily work in the Internet age, but there are ways to counteract and minimize damage.
- **Examine the broader need for a comprehensive communication and crisis management plan that incorporates the dynamic nature of the Internet:** Laying the groundwork now puts you in the best position to respond when something happens.
- **Suggest the ways in which a risk management practitioner can be proactive in communicating risks and possible strategies to senior management and others in the company:** Crisis management is, as always, a team sport, and getting buy-in from impacted individuals in the company is a top priority.
- **Provide additional helpful resources:** The threats presented here cannot be addressed and forgotten. They require ongoing diligence, and there are resources that can help.

Understanding Threats from New Internet Technologies

Companies should not underestimate the potential impact of social media on their business. Social media has tremendous power to do good—and harm.

YOUTUBE

Founded in 2005 and now a subsidiary of Google, YouTube is a video-sharing website. Most of the content on YouTube is uploaded by individuals, and registered users are allowed to upload an unlimited number of videos. Videos considered to contain potentially offensive content are available only to registered users over the age of 18, and YouTube's terms of service prohibit the uploading of videos containing defamation, pornography, copyright violations, and materials encouraging criminal conduct. However, YouTube does not screen the videos before they are posted online and relies on users to flag content of videos as inappropriate. According to the site's community guidelines:

> We trust you to be responsible, and millions of users respect that trust. Please be one of them .... YouTube staff review flagged videos 24 hours a day, seven days a week to determine whether they violate our Community Guidelines. When they do, we remove them.[1]

It is estimated that 20 hours of new videos are uploaded to the site every minute, and three-fourths of the content comes from outside the

United States. It has also been reported that YouTube garners well over one billion page views daily worldwide.

TWITTER

Founded in 2006, Twitter is a free social networking and micro-blogging service that enables users to send text-based posts of up to 140 characters called tweets. Senders may restrict delivery to their circle of friends or, by default, allow open access. Jane Jordan Meier, a crisis communication coach and trainer, notes there are many possible productive uses of Twitter; examples she cites include the U.S. Department of Labor, which uses it to distribute news; the Centers for Disease Control and Prevention (CDC), which provides updates and information during emergencies via Twitter; and the Los Angeles Fire Department, which tweets regularly about wildfires. Meier explains:

> Quite simply, Twitter is fast becoming the go-to place for instant and emergency communication as it reflects real-time information.[2]

Anyone in the vicinity of an emergency can provide field reports, and journalists can aggregate tweets as part of their reporting. Twitter can be a strategic tool for emergency communications and notification for business continuity. From a marketing perspective, companies can use Twitter to track consumer thoughts. However, the immediate nature of Twitter communications can present significant risks to a company. Obviously, the content of tweets is not confirmed or necessarily true, and yet they can be broadly and instantly circulated to thousands of recipients. Twitter is, in effect, a vast, uncontrolled and unmanageable media that can either cause a corporate branding or image crisis, exacerbate it, or prolong its effect as messages reverberate among thousands of Twitter users.

FACEBOOK

Incorporated in 2004 and open to everyone age 13 and older since 2006, Facebook is a global social networking website that enables users to add friends, send them messages, and update their personal profiles to notify friends about themselves. Creating a page on Facebook is easy, and a lot of unofficial corporate and celebrity pages have sprung up. Facebook is trying to make pages an integral part of its advertising products, so it wants the brands themselves to own their presence on Facebook, which means Facebook regularly takes unofficial pages and folds them into the official ones.

Facebook insists that "only authorized representatives may administer a Page for a brand, entity (place or organization), or public figure."[3] But questions of authentication suggest other legal issues: Is Facebook responsible for the accuracy of pages? To what degree are communities responsible for the entities they represent?

MYSPACE

Founded in 2003 and open to anyone age 13 and older, MySpace is a social networking site now owned by Specific Media, LLC. MySpace was the most popular social networking site in the United States until 2008, when it was surpassed in popularity by Facebook. Among the site's features is the ability to post messages on a bulletin board for everyone on a user's friends list to see. Some users employ bulletins to deliver chain messages about politics or religion, warnings about a bad consumer experience, Internet rumors, or negative information about a company or brand.

OTHER SOCIAL NETWORKING SITES

The short list above includes some of the most popular sites. On Wikipedia, users keep an always-growing list of more than 200 other social networking sites that could pose similar problems: http://en. wikipedia.org/wiki/List_of_social_networking_websites.

Examples of Internet-Based Incidents

Any risk management professional can immediately see the potential for these web 2.0 technologies to be misused to the possible detriment of a company or brand. However, often it is difficult to convince other business functions that hope to leverage web 2.0 (e.g., sales and marketing) to appreciate the possible risks. Here are some examples of what can happen when things go wrong and the company has no process in place to quickly respond.

DOMINO'S PIZZA

Three workers at a Domino's restaurant in Conover, North Carolina, thought it would be funny to make a video of them clowning around while making food. The video included apparent food contamination by workers. According to a report from *Advertising Age*, another worker narrated the incident:

> "In about five minutes, they'll be sent out to delivery, where somebody will be eating these, yes, eating them... That's how we roll at Domino's."[4]

The video was uploaded to YouTube and within a couple of days it had been viewed more than one million times, thanks in part to Twitter and other viral social media. The employees were fired and faced felony charges for distributing prohibited foods; they contended the video was a prank and the food was never delivered. At first, the company did not respond, but days later it became clear that the controversy was escalating. The company posted an apology on its websites and asked employees with Twitter accounts to tweet a link to it. The company also created a Twitter account to reassure customers, and its U.S. president issued an apology on YouTube. Even after the incriminating video was removed, there remained locations on the web where it could be viewed.

In response to the incident, *Time* magazine interviewed experts and suggested five ways Domino's could respond to this corporate crisis:[5]

- Create a blog on the Domino's website to help serve as a powerful rapid response vehicle.
- Tap into the company's most loyal customers and ask them via email to encourage their friends to support the company.
- Update the Wikipedia entry to include a link to Domino's executive response to the incident.
- Move aggressively to cancel out negative reinforcement of the incident in Google search results, including buying ads from Google to relay positive messages.
- Take a break from commercial advertising until the controversy dies down (Domino's decided instead to continue with a schedule of advertising).

Unfortunately for Domino's, the effects of the controversial video on its brand image were far reaching and long lasting. According to *Advertising Age*, Domino's quality and buzz ratings (as measured by BrandIndex) were especially impacted.[6] Buzz fell from 22.5 to 13.6 points, and quality ratings fell from 5 to minus 2.8. Additionally, prior to the posting of the video, Zeta Interactive's measurements showed Domino's buzz rating had been 81 percent positive; following its posting, however, that rating dropped dramatically, to 64 percent negative.

UNITED AIRLINES

When musician Dave Carroll looked out the window of a United Airlines plane on the ground at O'Hare Airport in Chicago and saw a baggage handler toss his guitar onto the ramp, it was the beginning of one of the more convincing examples of the power of viral YouTube videos to attack a company's reputation. Unhappy with United's response to his complaints when his guitar was severely damaged, Carroll and his Sons of Maxwell band wrote and recorded a video of a catchy song titled "United Breaks Guitars." After the video was posted on YouTube, it became viral and was subsequently viewed by millions (the latest count was more than 12 million views). The four-minute, 37-second video was entertaining and also played into general consumer frustration related to airline service, lost bags, etc. The lyrics of the song specifically mentioned a certain Ms. Irlweg who allegedly denied Carroll's claim for compensation because he didn't complain at the right place at the right time.

United responded with its own video and reportedly also answered some tweeted comments. To some extent, the company's response was lost among multiple fake responses posted on YouTube, including some alleging to feature Ms. Irlweg or a United Airlines official. After Carroll declined a belated offer of compensation, the airline reportedly donated $3,000 to the Thelonious Monk Institute of Jazz as a "gesture of goodwill." United's written response included the statistic that "99.95 percent of our customers' bags are delivered on-time and without incident, including instruments that belong to many Grammy Award-winning musicians."

The impact of the video continued long after it was posted. The incident has been featured on Fox News and CNN. Carroll followed up the song with second and third variations, and additional response videos continue to surface, including videos entitled "Hitler Finds Out United Breaks Guitars" and "Northwest Breaks Dulcimers." A corporate response from Taylor Guitars, which made the damaged guitar, also became available on YouTube. The *Times Online* reported that United's share price plunged by 10 percent four days after the song's release, costing shareholders $180 million. In December 2009, *Time* magazine named "United Breaks Guitars" No. 7 on their list of the Top 10 Viral Videos of 2009. To add further insult to injury, the video's publicity later resulted in a book deal for Carroll: *United Breaks Guitars: The Power of One Voice and the Impact of Social Media* was published by Hay House in 2012.

OTHER EXAMPLES

Brand Image Threat	Example
Web 2.0 media have no international boundaries	A Pepsi advertisement intended for the German market caused worldwide controversy when people took offense at its depiction of the lonely calorie in Pepsi Max committing suicide. Pepsi's apology emails and tweets also spread rapidly over the Internet, thus demonstrating the effect of social media on how brands and consumers interact.[7]
Employees may put a brand in danger when they engage in open conversation on the web	When one soon-to-be Cisco employee tweeted about deciding whether to accept a job even though he would "hate the work," and Cisco corporate replied to the tweet, the incident spun into a media blitz, including an MSNBC article and calls from Oprah Winfrey.[8]
Internal mistakes may turn into public embarrassment when the error affects products sold online	An online petition against Amazon.com was created when hundreds of gay and lesbian books lost their sales rankings on the mega-retailer's site, making them difficult for consumers to find. Speculation grew that Amazon was trying to suppress the visibility of gay and lesbian titles, even when they cited a simple "cataloging error."[9]
A company's perceived untimely response to consumer issues can become magnified when customers turn to social media to voice their discontent	Domain name registrar Register.com (which serves many small and medium-sized business owners) had a temporary failure as the result of a distributed denial-of-service (DDOS) attack. The resulting consumer frustration became public as people took to Twitter to spread the news.[10]

Planning Ahead to Mitigate a Possible Internet Crisis

Security should play a specific role related to mitigating Internet crises—a role that leverages security resources and capabilities in the context of an evolving threat to corporate well-being.

Specifically, the corporate security department should be well positioned to:

- Coordinate responses such as fact-finding, public–private liaison, interviewing, and addressing criminal and civil court issues, including restraining orders, prosecution, search warrants, chain of custody, and law enforcement involvement if an event has any criminal elements.
- Access and bring to bear resources related to various parts of the company, specifically based on familiarity with corporate and information technology (IT) interests.
- Marshal outside resources and contacts—such as investigators, law enforcement, profilers, and technicians—to help with a response.
- Tap into knowledge based on existing areas of responsibility related to protecting the brand, including planning for and responding to natural disasters.
- Work in cross-functional teams, a capability previously demonstrated in cases of workplace violence, counterfeit products, major investigations, and executive protection.
- Anticipate the need for any response to involve civil litigation, investigations, documentation, etc.

In general, security executives are tasked with planning and executing strategies for mitigating unwanted risks, including negative brand incidents on social networks. But before security take their concerns to management, they need to have an idea of how to assess the relevance of the problem to the specific business, which varies widely by industry segment. For example, in a branded food business, the possible damage is huge. It might be less so in another industry segment that is not as consumer-driven.

ASSESSMENT

A first step in assessing the issue is to reach out to colleagues to look for examples of others who have addressed similar incidents, especially companies in their industry group. They should look for success stories to emulate, and for experts in the field. This research can help direct the response plan, and should be guided by questions such as, "Could we respond quickly enough? Do we have pre-packaged video or other material to counter incorrect claims? Do we know how to interact with the systems?" It is a process to educate senior managers about the relevant issues, and if you have credibility with them, they will understand the process.

Security's responsibilities related to Internet crises are complementary to the responsibility of corporate communications to monitor what is being said and written about a company and the resulting impact on the brand. Corporate communications can monitor social networking sites or blogs for information and company mentions. The communications department is often tasked with responding to such information (and misinformation) on a day-to-day basis with the expectation that they will accelerate any response if an incident reaches a certain level of concern, and subsequently will turn to the crisis management team.

PREPARING FOR A CRISIS

Communicating with management is part of security's role. As part of the emergency and crisis teams, security should always be reviewing business-critical scenarios with upper management to manage risk. Tabletop exercises are useful tools to demonstrate how and why a risk situation might be addressed. When an incident occurs, there is no time to develop processes, roles, and responsibilities. These things need to be ready-made and already in place. A company's crisis management and business continuity policies may need to be modified to address this new kind of threat.

Crisis management teams should go through tabletop exercises three or four times a year to make sure that processes work. The exercises can include strategies related to addressing Internet crises. Companies need designated hitters ready to get on Facebook or other social media and respond right away. Designated employees in various subject areas should be ready to spring into action, pushing correct and relevant information into the various media and not just responding.

PROVEN RESULTS

Preparing ahead for a crisis actually shows a return on investment (ROI). Researchers Knight and Pretty have assessed how organizations responded to various mass casualty events, from 9/11 to the tsunami in Indonesia.[11] They found that the capital valuations of companies that responded well in emergency situations were much higher 18 months after an event than those of companies that responded poorly. While mass casualty events are obviously more extreme examples of emergencies, there may be a corollary value to having management prepared and on point in less tragic situations.

Research from the Aberdeen Group suggests that companies have every reason to want to catch issues related to the viral effect of social media at the first possible moment and to take appropriate action.[12] Aberdeen Group finds that today only 30 percent of "laggards," compared to 65 percent of "best-in-class" companies, are satisfied with their current ability to identify and reduce risk to the brand. At the same time, using online monitoring as an early warning system, best-in-class companies are 12.5 times more likely than laggards to experience year-over-year increases.

At the end of the day, any corporate crisis communications effort is a work in progress. It will always be a work in progress because the rules are changing so quickly. Furthermore, every company has its own culture—whether conservative, moderate, open, closed, pyramid, or flat—and how a plan of action plays out can be impacted by those variables. The most important thing is to have a plan.

When Time Matters Most: Responding in Real Time

After assessing the risk, security should determine ways to detect when an Internet-based brand attack has occurred and how the company should respond (and how fast). Security's role in crisis response is critical as an Internet crisis unfolds in real time. Having roles and responsibilities clearly defined beforehand ensures efficient use of time and resources in a crisis. When an Internet-related event occurs, time is measured in hours—not days or weeks. The immediacy of the Internet compresses time like never before, and companies must employ nimble new capabilities to coordinate their response.

There are three key factors to consider as companies seek to react effectively to an Internet crisis in real time.

SPEED OF RESPONSE

An effective response strategy has to include a reaction that is as fast as the Internet. Companies simply cannot wait to get their bureaucratic ducks in a row before addressing the substance and content of negative information online. Speed of reaction depends on the ability to convene all corporate team members to plan and coordinate a timely reaction to the crisis.

Plan how to get involved team members together in a physical "command center" or the virtual equivalent, whether it is a web conference or a conference call. A timely response to a crisis might include, for example, hourly (or even more frequent) updates on YouTube. And the response should come long before the exact details of how the company will handle the overall crisis are clear. It is much better to communicate what you know in a timely manner than to delay response until every fact is known or checked. For example, an appropriate response that would be possible early in the course of an unfolding crisis might be: "We have contacted the appropriate regulatory agencies to get them involved in the situation."

RELEVANCE

The nature of the response should be appropriate both to the content of the message and how it was spread. Matching the mechanisms, format, intent, and meaning of the response as closely as possible to the original message can maximize the benefits of a timely response.

An important strategy is to separate the incident from the norm. The company should be clear that "this is abnormal," that it is not typical of how the company does business. **Appropriate outrage should be expressed.**

A relevant response would also include launching an immediate investigation to confirm exactly what happened, making it clear in the process that an appropriate response will be forthcoming once the facts are known. A company should always spell out the actions they will take and the possible consequences for perpetrators (e.g., persons involved will be fired, they will be subject to possible regulatory sanctions or fines, or they will be prosecuted for violation of the Food Safety Act). Such responses can immediately transform the incident from a security incident to a possible criminal product contamination issue or at least a regulatory issue. If a company emphasizes denials and makes no comment, people will fill in the blanks in their own way.

The response should use the same channels and media that were used in spreading the original destructive content. If it was a YouTube video, the response should be a YouTube video. The corporate message in these situations is critical, and it can be a balancing act. Most important, the responding message should be credible. It should be targeted to the right level of understanding and the right entertainment texture. It should be neither flippant nor preachy. Videos of CEOs at their desks do not generate large YouTube audiences. By using the same search terms as the original content, companies can increase the chance that their response will come up alongside the original content in Google or another search engine. Phrases like "corporate response" actually make it less likely that the response information will be delivered in a search.

Finally, **any response to an alleged incident should express skepticism about the veracity of a claim or incident.** Using phrases such as, "if this really happened," can avoid appearing to confirm a false claim and at the same time leverage widespread skepticism among Internet users about any information that appears on the web. This strategy can also help to buy time.

It is important to assess the impact of what is being shown against the audience that might see it, and to be nimble in responding to put anxieties to rest: "We have reported this and have brought the authorities in. We are bringing additional quality assurance people into our locations. We are offering incentives to employees to report these situations. We have an internal hotline to encourage anonymous reporting."

Companies must take a proactive approach with this message: **"Our product is sacrosanct, and our goal is to provide the best product in the world. If anyone tries to harm our stakeholders, we will hold them accountable."**

CLOSURE AND FOLLOW-THROUGH

Putting out the fire is only the first part of the response. Subsequent efforts should involve the Internet crisis equivalents of both fire prevention and fireproofing of the brand and company. Again, it is important to leverage the same medium and channel on which the false claims were publicized to communicate what the company is doing to address the situation. Follow-through is critical as the investigation is closed out, and detailed information about the findings of any investigation should be widely reported and recorded.

In "closing the loop" on an incident, look for other stakeholders who can join the company in a united front. For example, sometimes it is helpful to find other stakeholders who could be damaged by the malicious attack to work together to communicate corrected information. A trade association might be concerned about industry-wide damage that could come from an attack on a single company. Also, involving regulators to take part in a joint statement can add credibility to the results of a finding. **Always look for a larger issue that is at**

stake, and one that the company can take a proactive leadership role to address. How can the company learn from the negatives of the situation and expand its role as an industry leader to address broad issues?

Announce a broad-based, far-reaching effort to solve the problems, and possibly fund a special research effort or other project to address the problem. After an incident dies down, Internet rumor services such as Snopes.com and other Mythbuster-type sites are helpful to avoid urban legend status, and companies should always monitor their Wikipedia entries closely to ensure that false information is not added.

When incorrect information is reported, it can be insidious. Once reported, it can come up again and again, and each time it can look like news. It is naïve for corporations to think that because they have defended against information once, they will never have to do so again. It will come up again, and it will have to be addressed. The possibility has to remain top-of-mind.

The drama of an event is sensational; the solution is often not. The solution will not get the same news treatment as the problem. Also, corporate executives should be prepared if a past incident is mentioned in a shareholder's meeting. They need to be willing to revisit the facts: "Here is where we are." Historical problems could also come up on the lecture circuit, so executives should always be kept up to speed.

A Comprehensive Approach to Internal Communications

Corporations should have sound policies and/or guidelines in place regarding how employees use YouTube, Twitter, Facebook, and other social media. They should specify clearly what appropriate and inappropriate use of proprietary information is. Security should investigate instances that are questionable, for instance, when an employee posts proprietary information or information about fellow employees. Companies must also recognize that, given the ubiquity of cameras, mobile devices, and free file-sharing services, they cannot possibly control entirely how information comes and goes from their location(s).

Effective communication in the web 2.0 environment relies on engagement; for example, if a blogger says something negative, a company representative could offer a response or ask for more information. Engaging people is a great way to establish a dialog. If you find a blogger who is writing about your company, it's a good idea to connect with him or her. Companies should be willing to put information and ideas out there, especially on blog sites that are becoming well known or that can influence consumer behavior. Strong brands get the benefit of the doubt. Also, the longer you have to build a strong brand, the better your bank account of good will; it will take more than a single incident to damage the brand. Elements of a comprehensive corporate approach to communications include credibility, constant monitoring, executive education, and rapid response to rumors.

CREDIBILITY

Security has the expertise and insight to evaluate information, identify omissions, and detect counterfeiting. It's important to realize that misinformation is often the omission of pertinent facts. Providing part of a story can be as misleading as outright lying. Security can help put the pieces together to ensure a credible and truthful message. Security is also aware that sometimes misinformation is driven by an agenda. If a group or person has intent other than what they advertise, security should investigate motives.

THE NEW TIMELINE

The transition to web 2.0 technologies requires the ability to respond quickly and depends on receiving early warning. Monitoring YouTube, Facebook, blogs, and other Internet venues is a key strategy to ensure early warning of a problem. Multiple entrepreneurial companies have emerged to offer services that do just that, and they are capable of finding offending information that might not show up in a typical Google search. Companies should employ constant monitoring, through either an appropriate vendor or a dedicated employee or department.

EDUCATE EXECUTIVES ON HOW TO RESPOND

Addressing these incidents is not an intuitive skill. Over the years, many corporations and other organizations have realized the need for their executives to communicate well on radio and television and have taught them how to effectively answer interview questions in these venues. Today the changing landscape makes everyone a communicator. It behooves organizations to react accordingly and to expand communications training to address the changing Internet environment. Communication is a currency, and the rate of communications has picked up at network speed.

DON'T LET RUMORS START

The Internet is full of conspiracy theories and rumors based on a kernel of truth. It is prudent for companies to look at themselves objectively. There are vulnerabilities whether you like it or not, whether they relate to how you do business, where you do business, or who your business partners are. A company's asset protection special-ist (security) should keep the management team well informed so that they can respond responsibly and accurately.

Managers should be able to say, truthfully, that they have invested millions of dollars into protecting and preserving their brand. If they have done so, the strength of the brand will make it easier to withstand the assault, and the public will be more likely to give the company the benefit of the doubt. Companies can actually gain from having han-dled a crisis well and with confidence, especially if they valued their people over assets and products. Protecting the company from brand damage risk is clearly very important. Security's role is to assess such threats and develop mitigation strategies in line with corporate strate-gies, whether they're long established or newly emerging.

Additional Resources

Domino's: How One YouTube Video Can Ruin a Brand, www.readwriteweb.com/archives/dominos_youtube_video.php

Domino's Pizza YouTube Video Lesson: Focus on Standards and Pack Your Own Lunch, www.businessweek.com/the_thread/brandnewday/archives/2009/04/dominos_pizza_y.html

For Companies, a Tweet in Time Can Avert PR Mess, http://online.wsj.com/article/SB124925830240300343.html

Pepsi Max's Bad Press, http://www.vanksen.com/blog/pepsi-maxs-bad-press/

Damage Control: Social Media Reversals, http://www.web-strategist.com/blog/2009/10/04/damage-control-social-media-reversals/

Perception Is Reality: Plan and Communicate Your Way through a Catastrophe, www.disaster-resource.com/articles/02p_101.shtml

'Beta Site' World: Building a Resilient Business, *Security Magazine*, www.securitymagazine.com/Articles/Cover_Story/BNP_GUID_9-5-2006_A_10000000000000131909

Consultant Ram Charan on Security's Role In Protecting Brands, *CSO Magazine*, www.csoonline.com/article/221344/Ram_Charan_The_Business_of_Security?contentID=221344

Critical Incident Protocol (CIP), Community Facilitation Program, developed by the School of Criminal Justice, Michigan State University (MSU), http://cip.msu.edu/

Transform—The Resilient Economy: Integrating Competitiveness and Security, *Council on Competitiveness*, www.compete.org/publications/detail/31/the-resilient-economy-integrating-competitiveness-and-security/

National Incident Management Plan, Incident Command System Overview, http://www.fema.gov/emergency/nims/IncidentCommandSystem.shtm#item1

ALSO AVAILABLE IN ELSEVIER'S SECURITY EXECUTIVE COUNCIL RISK MANAGEMENT PORTFOLIO

Information Security
Playbook
Forthcoming, September 2013

Managing Risks in Business
Proven Practices
March 2013

Media Exposure and Risk
Proven Practices
Forthcoming, June 2013

Research about the Attitudes on the Benefits and Controls of Web 2.0 in the Enterprise
Trend Report
Forthcoming, June 2013

The Benefits and Risks of Web 2.0 in the Enterprise
Trend Report
Forthcoming, June 2013

CONTRIBUTORS

Francis D'Addario, Security Executive Council Emeritus Faculty, Former Affiliation: Starbucks

Chuck Eudy, Security Executive Council Subject Matter Faculty, Former Affiliation: ING

Liz Lancaster, Director Member Services, Security Executive Council And several other members of the Council who wished to remain anonymous.

REFERENCES

[1] YouTube Community Guidelines. (n.d.). Retrieved from: http://www.youtube.com/t/community_guidelines.

[2] Meier, Jane Jordan. (2009, April 30.) Twitter: Ignore It at Your Peril. *Continuity Insights*. Retrieved from http://www.continuityinsights.com/articles/2009/04/twitter-ignore-it-your-peril

[3] Facebook Pages Terms. (2012, December 17.) Retrieved from: http://www.facebook.com/page_guidelines.php.

[4] York, Emily Bryson. (2009, April 14.) Domino's Employee: "The Cheese Was in His Nose." *Advertising Age*. Retrieved from http://adage.com/article/news/domino-s-employee-cheese-nose/135982/

[5] Gregory, Sean. (2009, April 18.) Domino's YouTube Crisis: 5 Ways to Fight Back. *Time*. Retrieved from http://www.time.com/time/nation/article/0,8599,1892389,00.html

[6] York, Emily Bryson. (2009, April 15.) The Aftermath of Domino's PR-Disaster Video. *Advertising Age*. Retrieved from http://adage.com/article/news/aftermath-domino-s-pr-disaster-video/136004/

[7] Edwards, Jim. (2008, December 3.) BBDO Airs "Suicide" Ads for Pepsi Max. *CBS Money Watch*. Retrieved from http://www.cbsnews.com/8301-505123_162-42740164/bbdo-airs-suicide-ads-for-pepsi-max/

[8] Popkin, Helen A.S. (2009, March 23.) Twitter Gets You Fired in 140 Characters or Less. MSNBC. Retrieved from http://www.msnbc.msn.com/id/29796962/ns/technology_ and_science-tech_and_gadgets/t/twitter-gets-you-fired-characters-or-less/#.UQbvAKugbkc

[9] Musil, Steven. (2009, April 12.) Amazon Criticized for Deranking "Adult" Books. *CNET*. Retrieved from http://news.cnet.com/8301-1023_3-10217715-93.html

[10] Krebs, Brian. (2009, April 5.) Web Sites Disrupted by Attack on Register.com. *The Washington Post Security Fix Blog*. Retrieved from http://voices.washingtonpost.com/securityfix/2009/04/web_sites_disrupted_by_attack.html

[11] Knight, Rory F. and Pretty, Deborah J. (1996). The Impact of Catastrophes on Shareholder Value. Retrieved from http://www.asse.org/professionalaffairs-new/bosc/docs/Catastrophesandshareholdervalue.pdf

[12] Aberdeen Group, Inc. (2009, April 4). Brand Reputation Management: Using Online Monitoring to Protect the Company's Crown Jewels. Available from http://www.aberdeen.com/Aberdeen-Library/5800/RA-brand-reputation-management.aspx

About the Authors

Bob Hayes has more than 25 years of experience developing security programs and providing security services for corporations, including eight years as the CSO at Georgia Pacific and nine years as security operations manager at 3 M. His security experience spans the manufacturing, distribution, research and development, and consumer products industries as well as national critical infrastructure organizations. Additionally, he has more than 10 years of successful law enforcement and training experience in Florida and Michigan. Bob is a recognized innovator in the security field and was named as one of the 25 Most Influential People in the Security Industry by *Security Magazine*. He is a frequent speaker at key industry events. He is a leading expert on security issues and has been quoted by such major media outlets as the *Wall Street Journal* and *Forbes*. Bob is currently the managing director of the Security Executive Council.

Kathleen Kotwica has a PhD in experimental psychology from DePaul University and has had a career as a researcher and knowledge strategist. Her experience includes positions as information architecture consultant at a New England consulting firm, director of online research at CXO Media (IDG), and research associate at Children's Hospital in Boston. She has authored and edited security industry trade and business articles and has spoken at security-related conferences including CSO Perspectives, SecureWorld Expo, ASIS, and CSCMP. In her current role as EVP and chief knowledge strategist at the Security Executive Council she leads the development and production of Council tools, solutions, and publications. She additionally conducts industry research and analysis to improve security and risk management practices.

About Elsevier's Security Executive Council Risk Management Portfolio

Elsevier's Security Executive Council Risk Management Portfolio is the voice of the security leader. It equips executives, practitioners, and educators with research-based, proven information and practical solutions for successful security and risk management programs. This portfolio covers topics in the areas of risk mitigation and assessment, ideation and implementation, and professional development. It brings trusted operational research, risk management advice, tactics, and tools to business professionals. Previously available only to the Security Executive Council community, this content—covering corporate security, enterprise crisis management, global IT security, and more—provides real-world solutions and "how-to" applications. This portfolio enables business and security executives, security practitioners, and educators to implement new physical and digital risk management strategies and build successful security and risk management programs.

Elsevier's Security Executive Council Risk Management Portfolio is a key part of the **Elsevier Risk Management & Security Collection**. The collection provides a complete portfolio of titles for the business executive, practitioner, and educator by bringing together the best imprints in risk management, security leadership, digital forensics, IT security, physical security, homeland security, and emergency management: Syngress, which provides cutting-edge computer and information security material; Butterworth Heinemann, the premier security, risk management, homeland security, and disaster-preparedness publisher; and Anderson Publishing, a leader in criminal justice publishing for more than 40 years. These imprints, along with the addition of Security Executive Council content, bring the work of highly regarded authors into one prestigious, complete collection.

The Security Executive Council (www.securityexecutivecouncil.com) is a leading problem-solving research and services organization focused on helping businesses build value while improving their ability to effectively manage and mitigate risk. Drawing on the collective knowledge of a large community of successful security practitioners, experts, and strategic alliance partners, the Council develops strategy and insight and identifies proven practices that cannot be found anywhere else. Their research, services, and tools are focused on protecting people, brand, information, physical assets, and the bottom line.

Elsevier (www.elsevier.com) is an international multimedia publishing company that provides world-class information and innovative solutions tools. It is part of Reed Elsevier, a world-leading provider of professional information solutions in the science, medical, risk, legal, and business sectors.